P.S. To the Beyond:

Communicating With (departed) Loved Ones

By

JHBaldus

P.S. To the Beyond:

Communicating With
(departed) Loved Ones

Published By
JHB Press of
Austin TX

Copyright   JHBaldus   2014

ISBN 0-9725215-3-4

Library of Congress Registration Number

TX 7-937-723

Cover Art Concept

And Original Sketches

By the Author

Contents

Acknowledgments 11

Introduction 13

1 About the hero 17

2 A message to his buddy 21

3 Messages to the author through others 25

4 The author's first direct interactive contact 29

5 Attempting contact - 4 concepts 33

6 The first concept 37

7 The second and third concepts 41

8 Last of the four concepts 45

9 Using the concepts effectively 49

10 Receiving messages 53

CODA Latest contact from the HERO 57

Epilogue - Possible communication with animals? 61

About the Author 65

Acknowledgments

Many people have contributed to this book-some knowingly/some unknowingly. The stories and communications are real, but have happened over a period of 22+ years. Some person's names I never knew and others are long gone from this plane or my records. To them all, I say "thank you".

I also wish to thank all who read this material and encouraged me to publish it. Most especially I wish to thank the genius, Bill Benitez, who transformed it into book format for both print and Kindle. He has my utmost respect and appreciation.

JHBaldus
Austin TX
July 8 2014

Introduction

On October 14, 2001 I published a booklet that I did not put into distribution. I had just spent 10 years working on a "real" book of my deceased son's music, lyrics and verse. (It is in the Library of Congress and for sale - bookstore - yet today.) I was tired of the self-publishing/ promotion business. Besides I had another major printing project in the works that went on sale in 2003. (It is transitioning into another medium, hopefully in 2015.) And yes, I am still tired!

However the other day I found myself wishing I could find the booklet. I was having a lot of fun with my website/blog. So, I thought it might be a cool thing, like writers in the 1800s did, to serialize the booklet and do it on the website. But it had disappeared in the my last move. Like many things in my life that I thought lost, yesterday I found it carefully shelved right under my nose. Of course I wasn't looking for it! Need you ask??

The topic could be considered odd, but in this day and age of mystical offerings (*Lost*), fantasy (Hobbit, anyone?) Syfy (Carry on, Mr. Spock) and *The 6th Sense* - I'm ignoring the recent and the gruesome - it may not seem as bizarre as it might have in 2001. It is about how to initiate communication from those of us who still live . . . to those who do not.

FYI - in HS chemistry I learned that energy is not lost, it only changes form. That is when I decided that the energy of a person, in other words their soul, never dies. Thus began my interest in the soul continuum.

Many people tell stories about how someone they loved who had died managed to let them know that they are still around and trying to communicate. But most do not know how to initiate communication from this side of the curtain, so to speak. That's what I plan to explain. Although this material began with my son, I did resist titling it "And He Still Won't Shut Up" (Kidding!) Here is the actual title of that original, self-published booklet:

P.S. To The Beyond: How to Directly Communicate with Loved Ones On the Other Side

I have updated, edited, and adapted the material to make it appropriate for Kindle and print in book form. I also re-titled it. However, the content and my intent to help others remain the same. May this information help you and yours find peace if or when you should ever need it.

One

Fortunately, I had seen the movie *Ghost* starring Patrick Swayze and Demi Moore with my only son (BK) before he died. Without that film I would not have understood the events that followed. He and I laughed over Swayze's attempts to move objects around (after his character had died). He was trying to get the attention of his wife (Demi's role).

It was clear that his efforts took a lot of energy and practice. BK marveled aloud at the concentration it seemed to take . . . and patience. Then one day he decided to find out for himself if it could be done. BK, who loved to compose, write lyrics, sing, plus arrange rock and roll music to play with his band, died on October 14, 1992 at the age of 30 . . . of AIDS.

I have always been nervous about ghosts or things that go bump in the night. But I learned at a young age there was usually a logical explanation for such sounds, such as an unlatched screen door banging against the house. Furthermore, I now understand that real ghosts are souls who have not yet found the guiding light back to the Source. They are trying to figure out their situation, such as in Nichole Kidman's movie *The Others* or in Patricia Arquette's TV series *Medium* based on the life of Allison DuBois of Phoenix.

What worried me more were poltergeists, those invisible, unpredictable entities that moved objects around. To my mind such activities were not to be believed, but if true, were the works of the Devil. However, I do not think that way anymore. I have come to know a loving poltergeist who at first could only get my attention by moving things around . . . my son.

For weeks after BK died I made compilation tapes for friends and family - many tapes. I spent hours deciding which of his 52 recorded originals should go on each of the three tapes. Then I made the masters, followed by dozens of copies of each set. I was obsessed over capturing his music, and his voice for all who loved him.

One afternoon I was trying to decide if I should make yet another set of copies, or stop. Suddenly, a new blank tape setting on top of the recorder, flew three feet over to the couch then fell to the floor. There were no tremors, no sonic booms, no wind gusts–nothing to knock that tape off. Plus, it did not just fall down or it would have landed at my feet. I laughed and half-jokingly said out loud, "OK! I get the message, BK. I'll stop." I did.

Then I forgot about it.

Two

Many months after BK's death, Robert, his buddy from BK's very first band came to visit me in Arizona. He was upset. He did not find out that BK had died until some time afterward. (We had tried to contact him, but could not reach him at the time.) During his visit Robert related a dream he had prior to BK's death. In the dream, BK asked Robert to meet him. The front room of the designated house was dark, but Robert found BK in the kitchen which was warm and well-lit. BK told him, "I am going away for a while, but I will be back. In the meantime I want you to take care of my family." Robert agreed, but was distressed that BK did not tell him more.

As Robert with tears in his eyes related his story to me, he offhandedly remarked that the kitchen had the strangest decoration. There was wooden trim around the ceiling with cut-outs of ducks in it. Shocked, I asked him to repeat what he had just said. What Robert did not know was - BK titled one of his last albums with the nonsensical phrase *Duck Baboo*. Finally I told Robert, "He wants you to play his music!"

At that moment, a smoke alarm hanging on a nail (while also setting on a plant shelf) came crashing down. It rolled around the corner, across another area and into the room where we were sitting. Then it fell over. "See, I'm right", I said. Robert and I burst out laughing.

These events did not bother me as one might suppose. I knew no one but BK could be responsible as I was the first person to own that house. Later it was difficult emotionally to sell the house because BK had visited me there. I could still see him taking a nap on the newly carpeted floor. However, I needed to be near Phoenix. So after living there 8 years (the longest anywhere ever) I sold it, moved and the active poltergeist activity stopped.

However, BK still wanted to communicate with me.   So, he took a new tack.

Three

One day several years after BK's death, I was working at a health care event with a lady I had met only briefly once before. We were set up in a drugstore but no one was around. Out of the blue she said, "Your son says to pick up the phone." Startled, I looked at her and said, "My son is dead." "I know," she responded, "but he says to pick up the phone anyway." The look I directed at the woman clearly indicated I thought she was crazy. But she paid no attention.

I had already been receiving unexpected messages from BK through various persons starting six months to the day and date after he died. On that day I was back visiting in Indianapolis. Even though due to my career moves, we had lived many places, including Chicago, we considered Indianapolis (Indy) our home base. "We" consisted of BK, his sister (my daughter) and myself. I had an appointment with a medium whom I had found very accurate and helpful when I lived in Indy.

I had an appointment with a medium whom I had found very helpful when I lived in Indy. (FYI - a medium is a person born with the ability to transmit information from the dead to the living.) When I called from Phoenix to set the date, I had an unheard bit of luck, I reached him on the first try.

During the session he reported that BK was sending me a message. The message was that BK had made it safely to the Light and the journey was "not too bad." The medium was amazed that BK could make contact so soon after his death. Nonetheless upon questioning it was clear that it was him, for real.

At about this time there was another message from BK but it was in the form of a dream sent to my cousin. He told her that he was "well and happy" in the afterlife. In addition, he had a phrase he wanted her to tell me.

She was concerned that since my grief was so raw, I would be very upset if I didn't understand what it meant. (It sounded like absolute nonsense to her.) But at the urging of other family members, she relayed it as requested. Happily, it did make sense to me. Thus, we knew the communication was really from him.

In subsequent years others volunteered information from BK as well. He made me aware with brief and rather generic messages that he was watching over us. However, as time went on he began to get more pointed in his messages sent through others.

On November 11, 1998 I was being guided in a visualization exercise while participating in a demonstration class. Afterward, our instructor asked if any of us had something to share. One of my classmates spoke up and indignantly indicated that she did. She reported she was having a lovely time dancing in a beautiful glade with her "higher" self and her "inner child" when a man walked in and said, "Tell my loved one to relax-stop trying to solve everything."

The classmate was irritated that a total stranger would intrude into her meditation. Furthermore she didn't know who the "loved one" was! I heard myself asking her to describe the man. It was BK. This event happened shortly after the drugstore incident. I had been puzzling over that message, since it still was not clear what BK meant by it.

Now, I was totally baffled.

Four

A few weeks after the latest message from my son, the phone rang 3 times then stopped. I ignored it, until I realized that had happened 6 times in 36 hours. My voice mail picks up after 4 rings, so there was no way the callers could have known they had made a mistake.

Suddenly it hit me. Pick up the phone! BK was trying to signal that he wanted to give me a message DIRECTLY! He wanted to talk to me one-on-one. But what could I do? I am not a medium (who can transmit info from the dead). . . nor am I a psychic (who accesses nonphysical information). How could I break the barrier??

It was a frustrating dilemma. My son wanted to tell me something and I did not know how to reach him. Sure, I prayed and sent him messages all the time. He in turn appeared in dreams - one very clearly remembered because it was a dark, cold night. We were talking under a streetlight. I reached over to tighten his muffler. (He was 6'2" - Adam Lambert without the bling resembles him.) He smiled and said, "There's more" and strode off into the night. I ran after him but he was gone and I woke up.

At this time I was taking courses in hypnotherapy at a private, accredited college. Various modalities that could be used therapeutically in conjunction with hypnosis were being demonstrated. I learned that a pendulum can be used to ask a person's subconscious for info that could help them. It also could be used to get guidance from those no longer in the physical. (A pendulum in this case is the name of a lightweight item dangling from a cord or chain, not the rod that only swings side to side in a clock.)

Right after class I went to the bookstore on campus. I had just enough money to buy a pendulum of my own. Once I was home I decided to try to contact BK. After praying, asking for protection and to receive only "true" answers, I asked if BK were present. He was! I asked if communicating using the pendulum was an acceptable modality for him (recognizing that it would take a lot of energy for him to move the pendulum). His answer was "Extcy". We had made direct contact . . . finally.

Prior to this I had tried "automatic" writing in an attempt to reach him. That is when a person sets a quiet scene and then writes down on a blank piece of paper anything that comes to their mind. (Some people can use their computers this way.)

However, I was always uncertain whether I was getting the correct message. So having the ability, using the pendulum, to check with BK directly and immediately appealed to me. He was willing to use this method from now on. Hurrah!

Five

For many years I had been told I would write a book that would help others. I had no clue what the subject should be. With my master's in Health Care and 40 plus years experience in the medical field, I thought it might be some lengthy tome on how to "fix" health care. (Actually it would be short and sweet . . . stop allowing self-aggrandizing competition in ALL components of health care! See?) However, I have become more and more aware of the destruction that pain causes. Not only physical, but most especially pain of the psyche can cause extensive damage to health and relationships. Easing such pain is my goal.

The purpose of this book is to help persons devastated by the the pain of loss of a loved one through death. The physical pain of severe loss is enormous and caught me by surprise. I had read of it, but both my parents lived years beyond my son. So I had not had any other death cause such a direct hit. Physically, it feels like a sword in the gut. It lasts about 2 years by my experience, verified by others. The pain to the psyche (the broken heart) caused by death's separation lasts a lifetime. However, I learned that the pain is less fierce once some sort of acknowledgement of the dead person's ongoing presence occurs. And if some sort of communication becomes available, the heart's pain is eased greatly.

John Edward with his TV program *Crossing Over* and public appearances/ private readings, as well as Doreen Virtue, PhD plus countless others, are serving as bridges of communication between those in the here and the hereafter. However, as effective as John and others (including the Long Island medium-Theresa Caputo) are, they cannot help every individual. This book was written to help you learn how to make contact with those on the other side.

There are four concepts to be noted here:

First, your loved one might not be present at the time you wish to ask them a question;

Second, any communication attempt should be approached with a calm and respectful attitude;

Third, praying can be instrumental in obtaining protection for your soul during a communication session and

Fourth, clarity of any request from you to your loved one is critical to receiving a relevant response.

Six

The first concept is - your loved one might not be present at the time you want to ask a question. If they are, they may not want to answer your question . . . at least not at first. This might be for your own good. In my case it had to do with reincarnation. (The ancient belief that souls can return to different physical lives as a way to learn universal lessons - from each new experience/ incarnation.)

I have long understood the idea that we are in the physical for a specific reason. I can still remember my preacher grandfather pounding the pulpit and saying, "We are in this life to learn a lesson!" (I was 7 at the time.)

About six months after BK and I had our first contact while using the pendulum, I was distressed over the possibility that he might be thinking of reincarnating into a family he had worried about when he was alive. At the time we were working out the details of his burial arrangements, (his idea to do it) we discussed the possibility of reincarnation. We both believed in the concept, but had no desire to test our beliefs. I did however ask him not to "return" while I was still alive. I did not want to look into the eyes of every baby I met and ask, "Is that you, BK?" He replied he would try not to. We left it at that.

I really wanted to know the answer to my question as the woman's due date was fast approaching. So I attempted to reach him. Once I knew he was present, I asked if he would answer that question. He indicated "no". I was frustrated. Then, I asked him if he had a message for me. He did. The message was "Prayers for me scrub the stuff off my soul . . . Thanks . . . I love you."

Well, at least I had an answer to that eternal question . . . do prayers make a difference? They do! I was happy, but still troubled. Did he, or did he not plan to reincarnate? So, I asked him again if he were willing to answer the question. He was. He did not intend to reincarnate. Months later I looked into the eyes of the infant in question. It was not BK. If he had answered my question first, I would not have thought to ask for a message. Just think what I would have missed.

Now, there are times when it is genuinely not in our best interest to know all about the future. We might make rash decisions that would affect the rest of the experience we need to have in order to learn a particular lesson. Also sometimes purely for our mental health, we do not need to know all. (We tend to get anxious.)

Also, on the topic of looking into one's future, do not get me wrong. I believe that we map out a plan for our life before we reincarnate in order to learn a particular lesson. I have no difficulty with a flashlight of knowledge being shown by a psychic on my personal road map of life so I can see where

I am. However, sometimes for our own good, we really do not need to know all.

A psychic friend of mine told BK indirectly that he would die at age 30. But she did not tell me because she knew I would not have let him out of my sight. . . and he had things to do without interference before he left.

He needed to get his music and his message out into the world. And so he did.

Seven

The second concept of the four that leads to a successful communication with a soul on the other side is to approach the session with a calm and respectful attitude. Praying, meditating or yoga prior to the session - any method a person chooses - is critical for opening communication channels. Being in an open, peaceful state of mind decreases resistance during communication. This is important since we are asking those who are elsewhere to come back to help us.

As you will read in books by authors such as Betty Eadie, Ruth Montgomery and Mary Summer Rain, people /souls can have occupations after they leave us. Do not misunderstand me, please. When a person is dead . . . that persona is dead to us on this side of the curtain, regardless of what currently popular entertainment vehicles would have us imagine. However, from what I have read and been told, there is a "somewhere" for souls to go (Heaven, perhaps?) And if they like, they can choose to perform helpful tasks.

One day a medium and friend startled me. She told me that BK's friend who died of AIDS two years before BK, was so relieved to find out there was a "somewhere" that he took a job! He was acting as an escort for others who died of AIDS. He helped them understand what had happened and that they were actually dead. Strange as it may seem, that knowledge is comforting to the newly deceased, I understand. They may not be happy about it, but at least they know where they are and why.

The third concept - obtaining protection for your soul during a session is critical and should not be ignored. Prayer can be instrumental . . . as simple as asking, "Please help me and give me divine protection. Thank you." Also, you can imagine yourself being protected by other methods. I like to imagine a laser-like white light of protection around me (from Obi-wan's light-saber?). It enhances the good and enables one to repel the not-so-good from tinkering with the communication. Another visualization is to "anchor" yourself by mentally running a golden cord from the top of your head down through the center of your body into the ground, thus binding yourself into the good earth.

Regarding communication with a loved one, be sure to state out loud that theirs is the only soul with whom you wish to communicate. There are others interested in assisting you, but you should not let them interfere with your communication. In fact I got a very stern message from BK once, warning me to only speak with him or other very close family members - no strangers!

Mischief can occur, as those who like to try Ouija boards can attest. You must make it clear you only want to hear from the soul with whom you asked to speak. Also state you will accept nothing but the truth!

Eight

The fourth and last of the concepts that are helpful for successful communication with souls on the other side is- the clarity of your request. Multifaceted questions or a question restated different ways can create confusing even contradictory answers. A question must be clear, concise and answerable with a "yes" or "no". It helps to write the question down as the answer will be to exactly what you ask, not to what you mean. (Even though they probably know what you mean or want, the answer will relate directly to the actual question.) Since you want to get the most accurate answer you can, the question must be framed carefully. Then it should be read out loud to be certain it is clearly stated. This will also give your communication partner time to research the answer if necessary.

Some helpful ways to state near future questions are to preface the questions with "Is it best for me if I do . . . ? Or Is it a good idea if I do . . . ?" Incidentally, you must be prepared for an answer you do not like. Remember that your loved one is in the "hereafter" and will be viewing the situation from a wider vantage point than you. That is why you are asking for their input. They have a perspective that is not available to you in the "here". So, take heed. And ask again later, if there is no answer at all.

Of course you will want to do everything possible to facilitate a satisfying communication. Remember, they will be draining their energy to give you answers. (Your energy will be decreased from this effort as well.) So, plan a quiet, open-ended block of time without deadlines for your conversation. I prefer to try to initiate communication late at night or very, very early in the morning. There is less human-generated negative energy in the air at those times. Also, I light a candle, usually white, and have it burning throughout to clear the air. Lights and fans are off. Pets and family are out of the area and of course phones are turned off. Concentration is better when one is undisturbed. FYI–a communication session can take as little as a few minutes, or as much as an hour and a half if you wind up having both questions and messages in the same session.

There are many methods your loved one may use to let you know they are present and wanting to communicate directly with you. Sometimes there may be the flick of a shadow. Other times it may be poltergeist activity, or maybe small miracles with meaning only to you and your loved one. Something unusual happening repeatedly may be a clue your loved one is trying to send you a message directly.

Messages often occur sporadically. There has been no pattern to the timing of BK's communications. They have occurred anywhere from three to nine months apart or longer. Other times they are just days apart.

The randomness of these communications can be unnerving. If you prefer, you could schedule appointments to meet on a regular basis. Or you could set a date and time for the next communication attempt at the end of each session.

Regardless of your approach, consult with your loved one by asking out loud if they will be available at the next date and time best for you. Use your pendulum to get the answer. Continue to ask until an agreed-upon meeting is set. Then, put it in your calendar and be on time!

Nine

Now we have covered the four concepts critical to the success of any communication with souls from the other side, namely: your loved one might not be present or willing to give an answer at the time requested by you; any communication attempt should be approached with a calm and respectful attitude; pray for protection of your soul before a session; and clearly state your question.

However, before we begin the process of learning how to use the pendulum to assist with your communication session, there is one more thing to note. Be prepared for the odd, even puzzling messages you might receive. Those on the other side tend to speak in metaphors and sometimes display a quirky sense of humor. If this happens, enjoy the joke and have a laugh with them!

Before you attempt communication using your pendulum, you will want to get comfortable working with it. Begin by establishing which way the pendulum will move for "yes". I suggest holding it at the top of the chain. Then say aloud "My name is _____(what it actually is). Remember which way the pendulum swings. Then say aloud "My name is _____" but use a fictitious name. Note which direction the pendulum swings this time. That should be the direction for "no". Be patient. It may take a few moments for the pendulum to begin moving since this is a new collaboration between you and it.

I suggest you practice by asking simple questions to which you know the answers to get in sync with your pendulum and feel confident that the responses are accurate. Some fun questions might be "Am I a millionaire?" or "Do I have a sister?"

Once you are receiving consistently appropriate answers and you feel comfortable with the pendulum you are ready to follow the four concepts.

Please note that at times the pendulum may not even move, or will swing in a circle. This could mean that: there is no more information; there is no answer available or more research is needed. If this happens, change the subject or wait a few minutes, then try again. If still no answer it just may not be the time to ask this particular question.

If the session is initiated by your loved one and you are expecting a message, prepare for it. Follow the four concepts just as you would if you requested the session. Since you will be receiving many words, it helps to have a pencil and writing paper available. Most of the time the message will be understandable if you have asked the soul to communicate in a language familiar to you. (A message in Olde English is of no use to you in today's world.)

Ten

To begin a message session, establish that your partner is ready by asking if they are present, just as you do if you are asking questions. A good way to start receiving a message is by asking how many words it contains. You may determine the correct amount by counting out loud from one upwards until you get a "yes" response from the pendulum. Be certain to leave enough time for a definitive answer. Remember, it can take a few seconds for the pendulum to change direction or even give a response at all.

At this point you need to state out loud that you are looking for the first letter of the first word. Then rather than going through all 26 letters of the alphabet, divide the alphabet into sections. I ask if the first letter is in the section from A through H. If the answer is "no", I ask if the first letter is found in the section I through Q. If the answer is still "no" obviously it will be found in the final section - from R through the rest of the alphabet. Once the section is identified, go through each letter in alpha order until you get a "yes" response. Write the letter down, then repeat the process until the word is completed. I suggest asking your communication partner (using the pendulum) if the word is correct before proceeding to the next one.

The process can become tedious, especially if the message is long. As the message begins to emerge, the session can take on aspects of a game of charades. You will find yourself jumping to conclusions. You may be right. However, using the pendulum, double-check. Your loved one may be going in another direction entirely.

Just as with anything else, working with your pendulum takes patience and practice. But you will get better at using it as a method of communication. Your intuition about what is being said will improve dramatically too.

However, if at any time you wonder if you are mentally influencing the pendulum to provide the answer you want to a question, stop. Restate the question. After a few moments, while your eyes are closed, make the pendulum start swinging in a circle to break the previous pattern. At the same time imagine you are "looking" at an all white movie screen.

Once you sense the pendulum has stopped swinging in the circle, open your eyes and see which direction it is going. The direction it moves should not have been influenced by you.

Finally, as you reach out to your loved ones you can be sure they are reaching out to you. Love and emotional connections never die . . . they continue, forever.

Good luck!

CODA

Yes, I am aware that CODA is a musical term that means "the end" placed in a distinct section after a repeated portion of a musical score. Since BK was/is a musician it seems appropriate here.

As I edited the previous material trying to cut down on the number of pages, I kept reading over and over how hard BK had tried to get my attention, including the pick-up-the phone request (in Chapter 3). Confession: I have not tried to contact him for an interactive session in over a year. I have mentally sent him messages, but that is all. Things have been so intense here on the ground, I haven't even tried. But as I

continued reading, I realized he was currently trying to reach me.

In recent weeks my bedroom phone had
been ringing every single day between
0800 and 0805. No message was ever
heard. Also, the frequency of the after-
noon/ evening random ringing (without
triggering the answering equipment) had
picked up. I assumed my number was close
to someone else's and ignored it. I forgot
that those on the "other" side are supposed-
ly able to manipulate our electronic equipment quite easily.

Well, it is with some embarrassment I must
report it was him. I know because I used
my pendulum and asked. Turns out he
wanted me to alert his sister about something. After a few seconds of trial and error
word-guessing, I finally decided he wanted
me to warn her about some danger having
to do with her car. Once I followed that
line of thinking, I got it. (The pendulum
practically leapt out of my hand as he sig-
naled "yes"–I had figured it out!) It was
great to have a two way interchange with
him once again. By the way, his warning
was timely and on target.

I hope that you found the information in this book useful and encouraging. Now you know that with practice, you, too, can share information with your loved ones on the other side. May all your attempts be successful but if not at first, keep trying.

One more thing, please remember to trust your gut (instinct). If any information you receive does not seem right or true, don't act on it. Wait and ask the question again at another time.

With all this in mind, I wish you clear, true communications . . . and peace.

Oh, and FYI - my bedroom phone has stopped ringing at 0800.

Epilogue

After reading *P.S. To the Beyond*, a business associate, a software engineer, called me to discuss it. This individual wanted to know if deceased pets could be contacted. The idea didn't seem too strange since I had recently heard of an animal "whisperer" (a medium who communicates with animals.) So, I answered that I hadn't tried. But it certainly seemed possible since we know that animals have souls. Ergo, they must also have some form of an afterlife that we could access.

We got together and reviewed the procedure for using a pendulum for this purpose. Then, after asking for protection; to speak only to the requested pet and to receive only true answers, my associate was ready with these questions;

1. ———— are you here?

2. ———— am I using your correct name?

3. ———— do you have two blue eyes? (The dogs were Huskies - one did have a brown eye.)

4. Did you like ———— (another dog in the pack)?

Answers from all (four) dogs obtained not by me, but by the owner of the pendulum, correctly identified each one. Pleased with the results, my associate left - determined to ask further questions later. Plus, I was informed, my associate was so satisfied with this technique that it is going to be tried as a method of communication with an alive animal, a horse . . . ?!

About The Author

The author is a medically-trained, scientifically oriented individual who has an expanded focus on activities that help people cope with their daily reality.

Since early 2013 the author's blog has posted thought-provoking ideas triggered by current events. As an experiment in self–publishing, this information was first serialized on that blog, *Unlikelycomments.com*.

While holding a BS (Ball State University), plus a MHA (Indiana University) the author completed the hypnotherapy program at the Southwest Institute of the Healing Arts, an accredited, private college in Tempe AZ and is a CHt (credentialed hypnotherapist) through the American Board of Hypnotherapy.

Formerly, the author was a hospital vice-president with expertise in Quality Improvement (QI) programs. This led to national and international consulting positions in hospital management and QI.

Now an entrepreneur, the author also has published books housed in the Library of Congress, plus developed and sold a (US trademarked) product used not only in the US, but internationally.

The author resides in Austin TX, USA

www.ingramcontent.com/pod-product-compliance
Lightning Source LLC
Chambersburg PA
CBHW071931020426

42331CB00010B/2819